REMARKABLE PEOPLE

Taylor Lautner

by Anita Yasuda

AV² by Weigl brings you media enhanced books that support active learning.

AV² provides enriched content that supplements and complements this book. Weigl's AV² books strive to create inspired learning and engage young minds for a total learning experience.

Go to www.av2books.com, and enter this book's unique code. You will have access to video, audio, web links, quizzes, a slide show, and activities.

BOOK CODE

Q1668

Audio
Listen to sections of the book read aloud.

Video
Watch informative video clips.

Web Link
Find research sites and play interactive games.

Try This!
Complete activities and hands-on experiments.

Due to the dynamic nature of the Internet, some of the URLs and activities provided as part of AV² by Weigl may have changed or ceased to exist. AV² by Weigl accepts no responsibility for any such changes. All media enhanced books are regularly monitored to update addresses and sites in a timely manner. Contact AV² by Weigl at 1-866-649-3445 or av2books@weigl.com with any questions, comments, or feedback.

Published by AV² by Weigl
350 5th Avenue, 59th Floor
New York, NY 10118
www.av2books.com   www.weigl.com

Copyright ©2011 AV² by Weigl
All rights reserved. No part of this publication may be reproduced, stored in a retrieval system, or transmitted in any form or by any means, electronic, mechanical, photocopying, recording, or otherwise, without the prior written permission of the publisher.

Library of Congress Cataloging-in-Publication Data

Yasuda, Anita.
 Taylor Lautner : remarkable people / Anita Yasuda.
     p. cm.
 Includes index.
 ISBN 978-1-61690-160-8 (hardcover : alk. paper) -- ISBN 978-1-61690-161-5   (softcover : alk. paper) -- ISBN 978-1-61690-162-2 (e-book)
 1. Lautner, Taylor, 1992---Juvenile literature. 2. Actors--United States--Biography--Juvenile literature. I. Title.
 PN2287.L2855Y37 2011
 791.4302'8092--dc22
 [B]
                                     2010007830

Printed in the United States of America in North Mankato, Minnesota
1 2 3 4 5 6 7 8 9 0 14 13 12 11 10

052010
WEP264000

Editor: Heather C. Hudak
Design: Terry Paulhus

Photograph Credits
Weigl acknowledges Getty Images as the primary image supplier for this title.

Every reasonable effort has been made to trace ownership and to obtain permission to reprint copyright material. The publishers would be pleased to have any errors or omissions brought to their attention so that they may be corrected in subsequent printings.

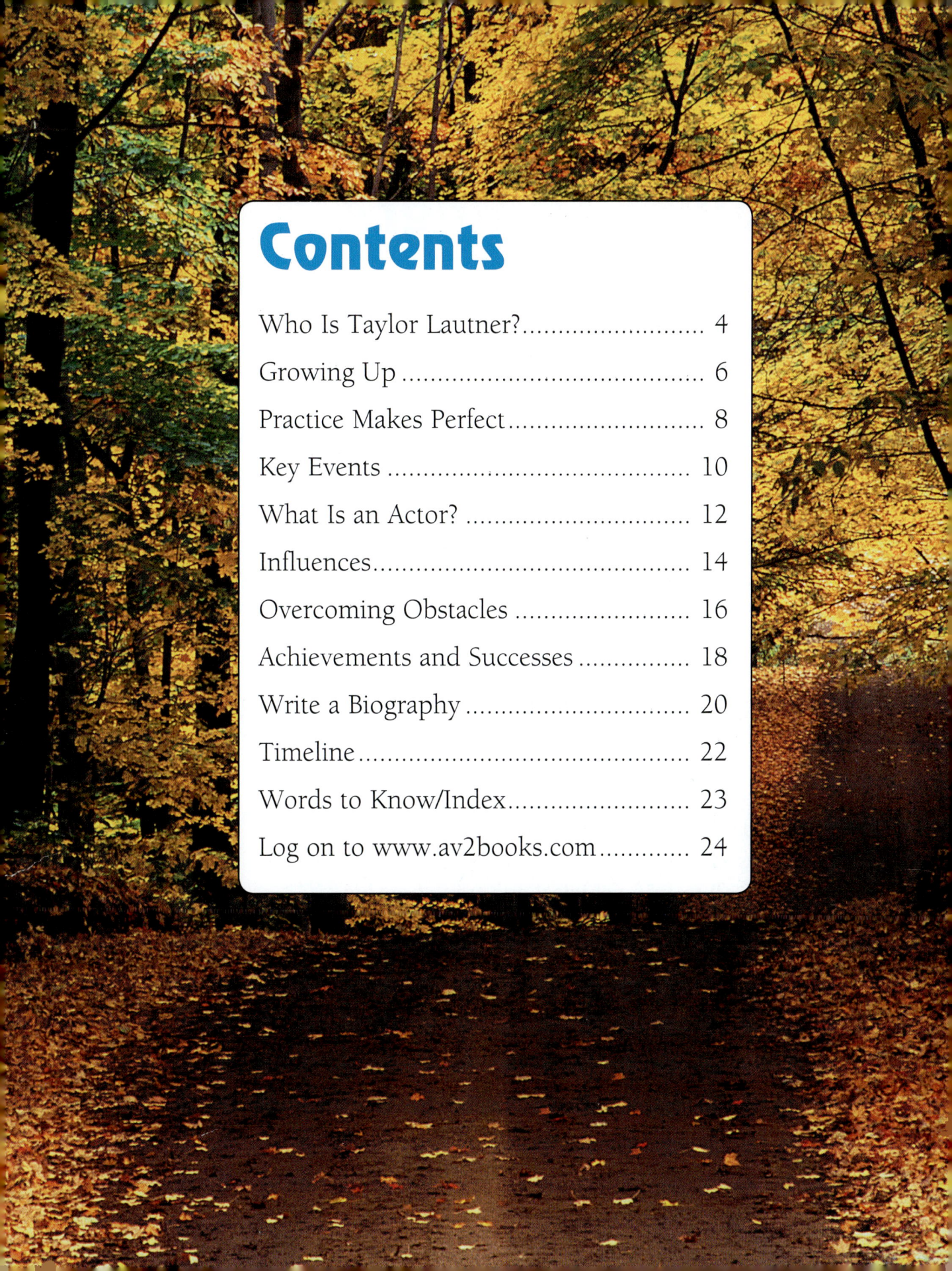

Contents

Who Is Taylor Lautner?............................ 4
Growing Up 6
Practice Makes Perfect 8
Key Events 10
What Is an Actor? 12
Influences 14
Overcoming Obstacles 16
Achievements and Successes 18
Write a Biography 20
Timeline 22
Words to Know/Index 23
Log on to www.av2books.com 24

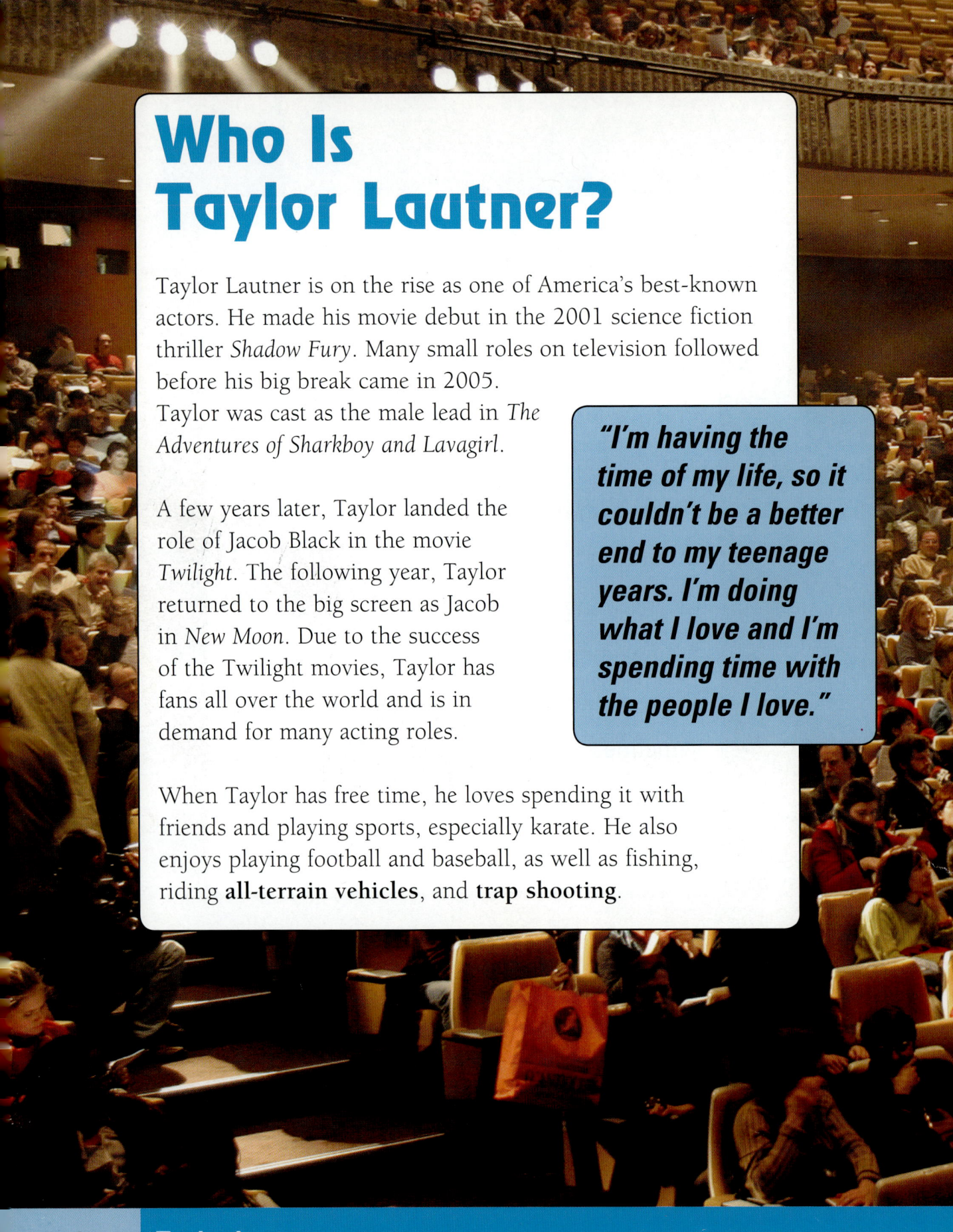

Who Is Taylor Lautner?

Taylor Lautner is on the rise as one of America's best-known actors. He made his movie debut in the 2001 science fiction thriller *Shadow Fury*. Many small roles on television followed before his big break came in 2005. Taylor was cast as the male lead in *The Adventures of Sharkboy and Lavagirl*.

A few years later, Taylor landed the role of Jacob Black in the movie *Twilight*. The following year, Taylor returned to the big screen as Jacob in *New Moon*. Due to the success of the Twilight movies, Taylor has fans all over the world and is in demand for many acting roles.

When Taylor has free time, he loves spending it with friends and playing sports, especially karate. He also enjoys playing football and baseball, as well as fishing, riding **all-terrain vehicles**, and **trap shooting**.

> "I'm having the time of my life, so it couldn't be a better end to my teenage years. I'm doing what I love and I'm spending time with the people I love."

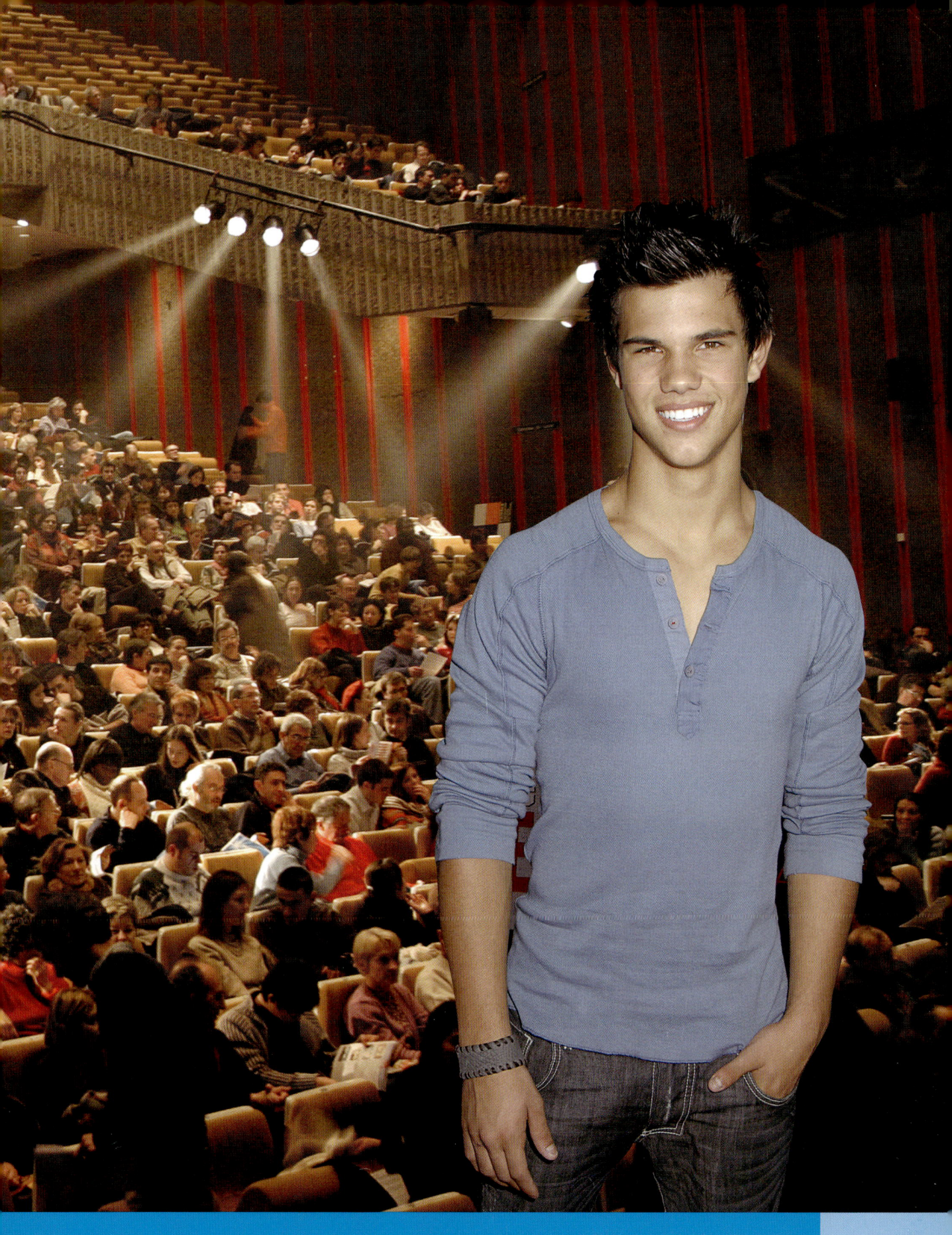

Remarkable People

Growing Up

Taylor Daniel Lautner was born on February 11, 1992, in Grand Rapids, Michigan. Later, his family moved to the small city of Hudsonville, Michigan. Taylor's father, Dan, is a pilot. His mother, Deborah, works for a software company. Taylor has one younger sister, Makena.

Growing up, Taylor loved sports. He is a natural athlete, and physical education was his favorite subject. At school, he took part in wrestling, baseball, and football. Taylor played running back and slot receiver.

At six years of age, Taylor began training in **martial arts**. By the age of eight, he was a World Karate Association champion and gold medalist. Taylor went on to win many more titles, including three Junior World Championships, by the time he was 12 years old.

■ Like his *Twilight* character Jacob Black, Taylor is part American Indian. His mother has Ottawa and Potawatomi ancestry.

Get to Know Michigan

ANIMAL
White-tailed Deer

FLAG

TREE
White Pine

Lansing is the capital of Michigan. Detroit is the largest city.

Henry Ford, inventor of the Model T Ford, was born in Dearborn, Michigan.

In 1891, the first international submarine railway tunnel opened. It linked Port Huron, Michigan, and Sarnia, Ontario.

The Detroit zoo was the first U.S. zoo to feature open exhibits. The cageless enclosures allowed animals to roam freely.

Many entertainers come from Michigan, including Madonna, Iggy Pop, Diana Ross, and Stevie Wonder.

Think about it!

Taylor became a karate champion and a successful actor at a young age. He had to work hard to learn the skills to become talented in both of these areas. What are your special skills? How do you work to improve these talents? How can you use these skills as a career?

Remarkable People 7

Practice Makes Perfect

When Taylor was seven years old, his karate instructor was Michael Chaturantabut. Michael uses the nickname Mike Chat. He is a well-known martial arts expert who has been in many films. Mike encouraged Taylor to **audition** for acting roles. Taylor's first audition was for a Burger King commercial. He did not get the part. Taylor soon began auditioning in Los Angeles for many roles.

In 2001, Taylor scored a part in the television movie *Shadow Fury*. The next year, his family moved to Los Angeles so that Taylor could focus on his acting career.

■ Taylor did voice work for television cartoons featuring classic characters, such as *Scooby-Doo* and *Charlie Brown*.

Taylor made his debut as a **voice artist** in an advertisement for *Rugrats Go Wild*. In 2003, he was cast for a TV role on *The Bernie Mac Show*. It was just six days before his eleventh birthday. Taylor continued to get roles on other TV series, such as *Summerland* and *My Wife and Kids*.

While Taylor was working on his acting career, he was also taking part in martial arts competitions. In 2003, he won the World Junior Weapons title.

By the end of the year, he was ranked number one in the world for his age by the North American Sport Karate Association.

QUICK FACTS

- Taylor played football during his freshman year in high school.
- Taylor is of French, Dutch, German, and American Indian heritage.
- Taylor has a Maltese dog called Roxy.

■ Karate is a form of self-defense that relies on strength, fitness, and mental awareness. Like Taylor, many people find that karate gives them the confidence they need to reach their goals.

Remarkable People

Key Events

In 2005, Taylor won the lead role in *The Adventures of Sharkboy and Lavagirl*. He received good reviews for his part in the film. Taylor's reputation as an actor began to grow, and he was cast in more roles.

After playing a few small roles, Taylor received the news that he had been cast as a main character in a major motion picture. In 2008, Taylor was on movie screens around the world as Jacob Black in *Twilight*. Though Taylor was in only three scenes, he was a memorable part of the movie.

Taylor had a larger role in the 2009 Twilight sequel, *New Moon*. In early 2010, he appeared in the romantic comedy *Valentine's Day*. Around the same time *Valentine's Day* was released, Taylor was cast as the lead in the upcoming movie *Stretch Armstrong*.

■ Taylor worked with actor George Lopez, writer-director Robert Rodriguez, and actor Cayden Boyd in *The Adventures of Sharkboy and Lavagirl*.

Thoughts from Taylor

Taylor's film roles have led to interviews in magazines and on television. He often shares his thoughts about acting, sports, and his other interests.

Taylor talks about getting into shape for a movie role.

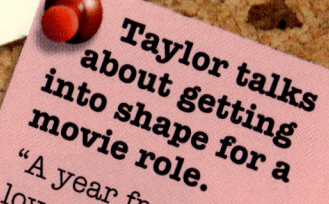

"A year from now, if I love a story and I love a character that requires me to lose 40 pounds, I'm ready to do it."

Taylor talks about the career he would pursue if he was not an actor.

"I always played sports when I was young. I played football and baseball for eight years. I loved football. So maybe I'd be doing some kind of sport."

Taylor talks about the popularity of the Twilight movies.

"Nobody really saw it coming. I mean, we knew we were making a movie of a very popular book, but we didn't know how well it was going to do. When it opened, it exploded, and that was not something any of us saw coming."

Taylor talks about his move from Michigan to Los Angeles.

"It was a very, very hard decision. Our family and friends did not want us to go."

Taylor talks about his character in the Twilight movies, Jacob Black.

"My character's very clumsy, outgoing, and friendly. When he transforms into a werewolf, he becomes something very different."

Taylor talks about what super power he would like to have.

"I like x-ray vision, like Superman, who can see right through things. I think that's pretty cool."

Remarkable People 11

What Is an Actor?

Actors play other people in theater, television, radio, or movie productions. They act out the movements and speak the lines of a character. Actors must show the feelings of their character in a way that seems real. They might change the sound of their voice or the way they look to do this. Costumes and makeup help certain characters seem real. Sometimes, actors train at special schools or work with a coach to improve their skills.

Some actors, such as Taylor Lautner, have other talents, as well as acting. They may be musicians, singers, or dancers. Taylor is an athlete. He often uses his martial arts skills in his roles. Many of Taylor's movies have included action sequences. In these roles, he must perform his lines and show emotion while throwing a punch or doing a martial arts move.

■ Taylor is friends with Selena Gomez and Miley Cyrus. Like Taylor, these actresses have talents other than acting. Both are singers.

Actors 101

Kristen Stewart (1990–)

Kristen is an actor who was discovered at the age of eight in a school production. In her first major acting role, Kristen starred with Jodi Foster in 2002's *Panic Room*. Kristen has appeared in more than 20 films. She is best known for her role as Bella Swan in the Twilight movies. She has been **nominated** and won many awards for her acting. In 2009, Kristen won the MTV Movie Award for Best Female Performance.

Miley Cyrus (1992–)

Miley is an actor, singer, and songwriter. In 2001, Miley landed her first acting job. Her movie debut soon followed in *Big Fish*. Miley auditioned for *Hannah Montana* when she was 11 years old but was turned down for the role. She kept trying, and a year later, she was given the role. In 2008, *Time Magazine* named Miley one of the 100 Most Influential People in the World. Miley's song *The Climb* from *Hannah Montana: The Movie* won her the 2009 MTV Movie Award for Best Song From a Movie.

Demi Lovato (1992–)

Demi is an actor, songwriter, and singer. As a child, she starred in *Barney & Friends*. Demi starred with the Jonas Brothers in the Disney Channel movie *Camp Rock*. Her first album, *Don't Forget*, debuted at number two on the Billboard charts. In the summer of 2008, she toured with the Jonas brothers. In 2009, she starred with Selena Gomez in the television movie *Princess Protection Program*. She won the Teen Choice award in 2009 for Choice TV Breakout Star. The same year, her second album, *Here We Go Again*, debuted at number one on the Billboard charts.

Zac Efron (1987–)

Zac first started his acting career in 1994 with an appearance on the TV show *ER*. Though he had small roles on many other shows, Zac became well known in 2006 when he appeared as the lead male character in Disney's TV movie *High School Musical*. Zac sang many of the songs that became hit singles from the movie's soundtrack. He was the first new artist to have two songs debut on the Billboard Hot 100 at the same time. Zac made the leap from TV to big-screen movies. He appeared in the musical *Hairspray*. Since then, he has starred in many more movies.

Motion-picture Cameras
Motion-picture cameras are used to film the action that appears in movies and on television. One of the first motion-picture cameras was developed by Louis Le Prince in 1888. This camera is on display at the National Media Museum in England. Today, motion-picture cameras use the latest technology to record film scenes.

Remarkable People 13

Influences

Taylor's parents have always supported their son's dream of working as an actor. Taylor's father, Dan, encouraged his son to try out for acting roles. Later, Dan acted as Taylor's **chaperone** on the set of *New Moon*. The entire family moved to California so that Taylor could launch his career. Taylor's parents have worked hard to help their son maintain a regular lifestyle despite being in the public eye. Taylor has an allowance and does chores.

Taylor enjoys watching action movies and dramas. Mark Wahlberg is one of Taylor's favorite actors. Mark started his career as a hip-hop artist. Today, Mark is known for his work in both dramatic and action movies. Some of his best-known movies are *The Italian Job*, *The Departed*, and *The Lovely Bones*.

■ Mark Wahlberg received an Academy Award nomination for his role in *The Departed*.

Matt Damon is another of Taylor's favorite actors. Matt became a well-known actor when he won the Best Original Screenplay Academy Award for the drama *Good Will Hunting*. Matt wrote the movie with his good friend and fellow actor Ben Affleck. He also starred as the title character, Will Hunting. Since then, Matt has starred in many action and dramatic movies, including the successful action series about the character Jason Bourne. Like Matt, Taylor has said that he would like to one day write movies.

THE LAUTNER FAMILY

Taylor lives with his family near Los Angeles, California. He has a strong bond with his father, Dan, who accompanies Taylor on movie sets. Taylor and his father often attend football games together. The pair are big fans of the Michigan Wolverines. Taylor and Dan also own a production company together. It is called Tailor Made Entertainment.

■ Even though they are rarely seen on the red carpet, Taylor's family often attends his movie premieres.

Remarkable People 15

Overcoming Obstacles

For years, the Lautner family flew from Michigan to California for Taylor's auditions. Often, the family had little notice about upcoming auditions. They could not prepare in advance for trips. After an audition, the Lautners would try to fly home early in the day so that Taylor could attend school.

It was a challenge for Taylor to balance school, football, martial arts, and acting. Taylor's hard work impressed his family. They agreed to try living in Los Angeles for one month to help Taylor further his acting career.

■ Taylor participated in the Los Angeles hip-hop group the LA Hip Kids. In 2005, he showed off his dancing skills at the premiere of the movie *Sahara*.

While living in Los Angeles, Taylor went to many auditions, but he was not selected for any roles. At the end of the family's trial month, Taylor got his first **callback**. Though he still did not land the role, he was motivated to keep trying out for parts.

By 2002, the Lautner family had moved to Los Angeles permanently. This was a very hard decision for the family. They had to leave behind other family members and friends in Michigan. However, Taylor soon started getting acting roles.

Even after his success in *Twilight*, the director of *New Moon* was not certain that he wanted Taylor to be in the movie. Taylor's character grows in height and gains a great deal of weight in *New Moon*. Taylor had to change his body for the role. He gained more than 30 pounds (13 kilograms) and worked out five days a week to bulk up his body. The director rewarded Taylor's hard work by casting him again as Jacob Black.

■ Taylor eats a healthy diet to keep his body in top physical form. One of his favorite meals is sushi.

Remarkable People 17

Achievements and Successes

Though Taylor has only been acting for a short time, he has received many honors for his roles. He was nominated for a Young Artist Award in 2006 for his work in *The Adventures of Sharkboy and Lavagirl*. In the movie, Taylor **choreographed** his own fight scene. People in the industry were impressed by Taylor's ability to act, dance, and do martial arts moves. Months later, Taylor won the part of Eliot in *Cheaper by The Dozen 2*.

The Twilight movies have broken box-office records around the world, earning large amounts of money. Taylor's role as Jacob Black has helped make these movies successful. T-shirts, dolls, games, bags, calendars, and many other items have been made of Taylor and his character, Jacob. Taylor has been given awards for his work in the Twilight movies.

■ Taylor took part in the 4th Annual DIRECTV Celebrity Beach Bowl in 2010.

In 2009, he was nominated for the MTV Movie Award Breakthrough Performance by a Male. He won the Teen Choice Award for Fresh Face Male the same year. In 2010, Taylor won the Nickelodeon Kids' Choice Award for Favorite Movie Actor, as well as for Cutest Couple, with *New Moon* co-star Kristen Stewart.

In 2009, Taylor hosted *Saturday Night Live*. In addition, he has been featured on magazine covers around the world.

HELPING OTHERS

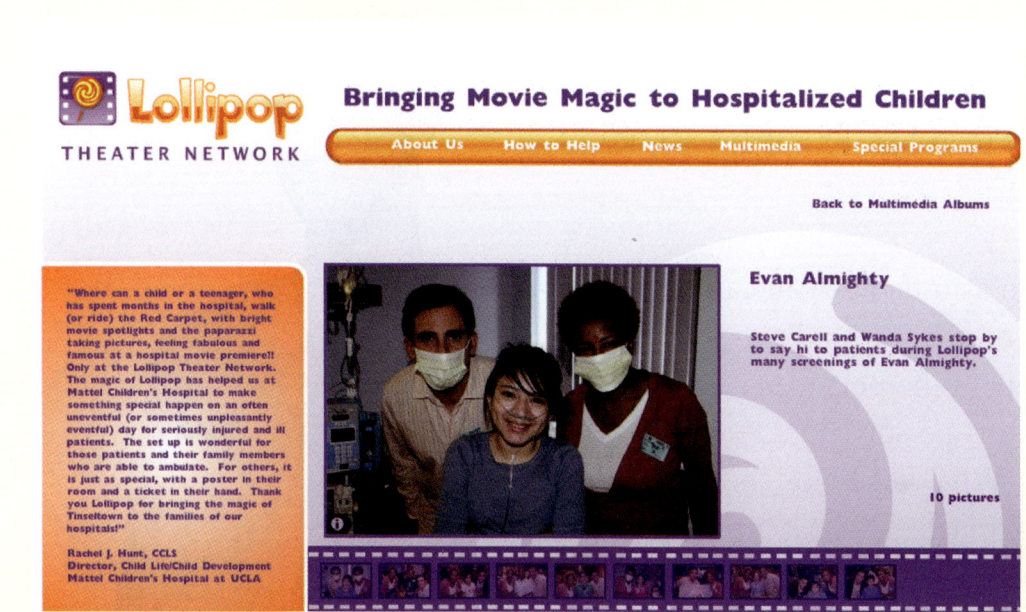

Often, actors use their popularity to increase public awareness of a certain cause. They may bring attention to nonprofit organizations and environmental efforts or help fund special causes. Taylor is involved with several **charities**, such as Hope for Haiti and the Lollipop Theater Network. Following the earthquake that devastated Haiti early in 2010, entertainers worked together to help raise funds for the nation. Taylor helped answer phone calls during the Hope for Haiti relief telethon. The Lollipop Theater Network is committed to improving the lives of people with an illness. The network brings movie experiences to children who are **chronically** ill or have life-threatening illnesses. Celebrity ambassadors, such as Taylor, attend movie screenings and pay in-hospital visits to kids. To learn more about the Lollipop Theater Network, visit **www.lollipoptheater.org**.

Write a Biography

A person's life story can be the subject of a book. This kind of book is called a biography. Biographies describe the lives of remarkable people, such as those who have achieved great success or have done important things to help others. These people may be alive today, or they may have lived many years ago. Reading a biography can help you learn more about a remarkable person.

At school, you might be asked to write a biography. First, decide whom you want to write about. You can choose an actor, such as Taylor Lautner, or any other person you find interesting. Then, find out if your library has any books about this person.

Learn as much as you can about him or her. Write down the key events in the person's life. What was this person's childhood like? What has he or she accomplished? What are his or her goals? What makes this person special or unusual?

A concept web is a useful research tool. Read the questions in the following concept web. Answer the questions in your notebook. Your answers will help you write your biography.

Taylor Lautner

Remarkable People 21

Timeline

YEAR	TAYLOR LAUTNER	WORLD EVENTS
1992	Taylor Lautner is born.	Johnny Carson hosts *The Tonight Show* for the last time.
2003	Taylor first appears in *The Bernie Mac Show*.	*Chicago* wins the Academy Award for Best Picture.
2004	Taylor makes an appearance on the show *Summerland*.	Sean Penn wins the Academy Award for Best Actor.
2005	Taylor plays the lead in *The Adventures of Sharkboy and Lavagirl*.	Dakota Fanning wins Best Frightened Performance at the MTV Movie Awards.
2008	Taylor stars as Jacob Black in *Twilight*.	*Ratatouille* wins the Academy award for Best Animated Picture.
2009	Taylor stars once again as Jacob Black in *New Moon*.	Miley Cyrus's *The Climb* wins the MTV Movie award for Best Song from a Movie.
2010	Taylor stars as Jacob Black in *Eclipse*.	Sandra Bullock wins the Best Actress Academy Award for her role in *The Blind Side*.

Words to Know

all-terrain vehicles: vehicles with three or four wheels that are used to ride over rough land and through water

audition: perform to try to get a job in the entertainment industry

callback: to be asked to return for a second audition

chaperone: a person who accompanies someone to look after them

charities: groups that raise money to help others

choreographed: created specific moves and steps to perform

chronically: lasts for a long time or happens repeatedly

martial arts: forms of self-defense that teach people to protect themselves using their hands, arms, feet, legs, and body

nominated: added to a list of people who will be considered for awards

trap shooting: competitive clay pigeon shooting

voice artist: a person who provides the voice for an animated character

Index

Adventures of Sharkboy and Lavagirl 4, 10, 18, 22

Cyrus, Miley 12, 13, 22

Damon, Matt 15

Efron, Zac 13

karate 4, 6, 7, 8, 9

Lovato, Demi 13

martial arts 6, 7, 8, 9, 12, 16, 18

New Moon 4, 10, 14, 17, 19, 22

Shadow Fury 4, 8

Stewart, Kristen 13, 19

Twilight 4, 6, 8, 9, 10, 11, 13, 17, 18, 19, 22

Wahlberg, Mark 14

Remarkable People 23

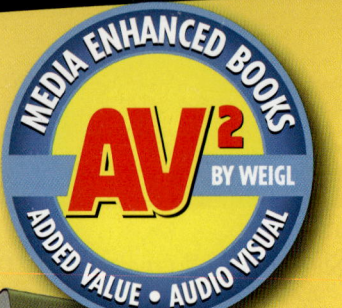

Log on to www.av2books.com

AV² by Weigl brings you media enhanced books that support active learning. Go to **www.av2books.com**, and enter the special code inside the front cover of this book. You will gain access to enriched and enhanced content that supplements and complements this book. Content includes video, audio, web links, quizzes, a slide show, and activities.

Audio
Listen to sections of the book read aloud.

Video
Watch informative video clips.

Web Link
Find research sites and play interactive games.

Try This!
Complete activities and hands-on experiments.

WHAT'S ONLINE?

Try This!
Complete activities and hands-on experiments.

Pages 6-7 Complete an activity about your childhood.

Pages 10-11 Try this activity about key events.

Pages 16-17 Complete an activity about overcoming obstacles.

Pages 20-21 Write a biography.

Page 22 Try this timeline activity.

Web Link
Find research sites and play interactive games.

Pages 8-9 Learn more about Taylor Lautner's life.

Pages 14-15 Find out more about the people who influenced Taylor Lautner.

Pages 18-19 Learn more about Taylor Lautner's achievements.

Pages 20-21 Check out this site about Taylor Lautner.

Video
Watch informative video clips.

Pages 4-5 Watch a video about Taylor Lautner.

Pages 12-13 Check out a video about Taylor Lautner.

EXTRA FEATURES

Audio
Hear introductory audio at the top of every page.

Key Words
Study vocabulary, and play a matching word game.

Slide Show
View images and captions, and try a writing activity.

AV² Quiz
Take this quiz to test your knowledge

Due to the dynamic nature of the Internet, some of the URLs and activities provided as part of AV² by Weigl may have changed or ceased to exist. AV² by Weigl accepts no responsibility for any such changes. All media enhanced books are regularly monitored to update addresses and sites in a timely manner. Contact AV² by Weigl at 1-866-649-3445 or av2books@weigl.com with any questions, comments, or feedback.